Tarts

Tarts

Jimmy Chok

Dedication

To my children, Javan and Joey, for just being themselves.

Acknowledgements

Thank you to the team at Marshall Cavendish International (Asia) Pte Ltd, namely David Yip, for giving me this opportunity to do another cookbook, and Lydia Leong and Lynn Chin for their part in working on this lovely cookbook. Thanks also to Elements by the Box for their superb photography skills.

Designer   : Lynn Chin Nyuk Ling
Photographer : Joshua Tan, Elements By The Box

First published as Bite: Tarts to Satisfy Every Craving, 2007
This new edition 2011

Copyright © 2007 Marshall Cavendish International (Asia) Private Limited

Published by Marshall Cavendish Cuisine
An imprint of Marshall Cavendish International
1 New Industrial Road, Singapore 536196

All rights reserved

No part of this publication may be reproduced, stored in a retrieval system or transmitted, in any form or by any means, electronic, mechanical, photocopying, recording or otherwise, without the prior permission of the copyright owner. Request for permission should be addressed to the Publisher, Marshall Cavendish International (Asia) Private Limited, 1 New Industrial Road, Singapore 536196. Tel: (65) 6213 9300, fax: (65) 6285 4871.
E-mail: genref@sg.marshallcavendish.com Online bookstore: http://www.marshallcavendish.com.

Limits of Liability/Disclaimer of Warranty: The Author and Publisher of this book have used their best efforts in preparing this book. The Publisher makes no representation or warranties with respect to the contents of this book and is not responsible for the outcome of any recipe in this book. While the Publisher has reviewed each recipe carefully, the reader may not always achieve the results desired due to variations in ingredients, cooking temperatures and individual cooking abilities. The Publisher shall in no event be liable for any loss of profit or any other commercial damage, including but not limited to special, incidental, consequential, or other damages.

Other Marshall Cavendish Offices:

Marshall Cavendish International. PO Box 65829 London EC1P 1NY, UK • Marshall Cavendish Corporation. 99 White Plains Road, Tarrytown NY 10591-9001, USA • Marshall Cavendish International (Thailand) Co Ltd. 253 Asoke, 12th Flr, Sukhumvit 21 Road, Klongtoey Nua, Wattana, Bangkok 10110, Thailand • Marshall Cavendish (Malaysia) Sdn Bhd, Times Subang, Lot 46, Subang Hi-Tech Industrial Park, Batu Tiga, 40000 Shah Alam, Selangor Darul Ehsan, Malaysia

Marshall Cavendish is a trademark of Times Publishing Limited

National Library Board Singapore Cataloguing in Publication Data

Chok, Jimmy, 1970-
Tarts / Jimmy Chok. – Singapore : Marshall Cavendish Cuisine, c2011.
p. cm. ISBN : 978-981-4346-58-0

1. Pies. 2. Pastry. I. Title.

TX773 641.8652 -- dc22   OCN704473925

Printed in Singapore by KWF Printing Pte Ltd

Contents

preface *11*

shortcrust pastry *12*

puff pastry *46*

filo pastry *76*

vegetable and other bases *98*

chocolate and biscuit bases *120*

basic recipes *138*

weights and measures *144*

Preface

It was only in 2002, after I opened my own restaurant, that I started to develop my interest in baking. I did not have much of a choice then, as I was running the business single-handedly and could not find good pastry staff. Out of necessity, I began to do more research on pastry and baking, and soon fell in love with the art.

I read cookbooks and magazines to learn more, and started to experiment by putting new ingredients together to come up with interesting combinations and dishes in my own style. These had to be dishes which I could serve at the restaurant.

Although it sounds easy now, the learning experience was not without any setbacks. Some of the recipes I tried looked promising when I was working on them, but did not turn out well after baking. But the amazing thing about baking is that once you have tried the recipe, you also start to understand the science of it—how it works—and so you can use the knowledge to improve on it until the final result is exactly as you imagined it to be, or even better!

So, to the novice cook, keep on trying. Put in a little of your own touch to these recipes whenever you set out to cook. Always be open to ideas and feel free to experiment with ingredients, flavours and textures.

To the seasoned cook, these are some of my favourite recipes which I hope you will enjoy. Although they are simple to do, they should get the conversation going at any party. Why spend hours labouring over the stove when you can easily prepare these attractive dishes at a moment's notice?

For those who prefer to make work even easier, frozen shortcrust and puff pastries are available from many supermarkets today. And for those who want to go a step further, ready-made crusts for tarts are also available at baking supply stores. Just buy a small quantity and have a taste to make sure you like it before buying more. Except for being convenient, ready-made crusts may not always rate high on taste.

I hope this book will go a long way in giving you a head start to your very own baking adventure!

Happy baking and *bon appétit!*

Jimmy Chok

Shortcrust Pastry

Fresh Fig Custard Tarts *14*

Pecan Tarts *17*

Panna Cotta Tartlets *18*

Passion Fruit Tarts *21*

Lemon Tart *22*

Lemon Curd Tartlets *25*

Assorted Mini Fruit Tartlets *26*

Baked Unagi Tarts *29*

Free-form Braised Leek Tart *30*

Marinated Herring and Chive Cream Tarts *33*

Cherry Tomato Balsamic Tarts *34*

Mushroom Ragout Tarts *37*

Salad Niçoise Tarts *38*

Free-form Port Wine-caramelised Shallot Tart *41*

Tomato and Mozzarella Tart *42*

Smoked Salmon Tarts with Gherkins *45*

Fresh Fig Custard Tarts

Fresh figs atop vanilla-scented custard. Enough said. Simply enjoy!

Shortcrust pastry	**1 quantity (see pg 140)**
Custard	**150 ml (5 fl oz) (see pg 26)**
Figs	**2, cut into wedges**

Preheat oven to 180°C (350°F).

Roll pastry out on a floured surface to about 0.3-cm ($1/8$-in) thick.

Line the base and sides of 4–6 medium tart tins with pastry and trim edges to neaten. Fill with beans, rice or baking weights. Alternatively, mould pastry by hand and place loosely over 4–6 medium tart tins for free-form tarts. Bake for 12–15 minutes or until golden brown. Remove weights, if used, and leave tart shells to cool slightly.

Spoon custard into tart shells and top with cut figs. Serve warm.

Makes 4–6 medium tarts

Pecan Tarts

Pecan tarts are an all-time favourite. The secret to a good pecan tart is in roasting the nuts, so they add extra crunch to the finished tart!

Shortcrust pastry	1 quantity (see pg 140)
Brown sugar	250 g (9 oz)
Salt	$1/8$ tsp
Butter	2 Tbsp, softened
Vanilla essence	1 Tbsp
Eggs	2, lightly beaten
Pecan nuts	250 g (9 oz), roasted

Preheat oven to 180°C (350°F).

Roll pastry out on a floured surface to about 0.3-cm ($1/8$-in) thick.

Line the base and sides of 4 medium tart tins with pastry and trim edges to neaten. Fill with beans, rice or baking weights and bake for 12–15 minutes or until golden brown. Remove weights and leave tart shells to cool slightly. Keep oven heated.

Combine brown sugar, salt, butter and vanilla essence in a mixing bowl. Add lightly beaten eggs and stir until well mixed.

Place half the pecan nuts evenly into tart shells and spoon mixture over. Top with remaining pecan nuts and bake for about 20 minutes or until filling is set. Test by inserting the tip of a knife into the centre of the tart. If the knife comes out clean, the tart is ready. If not, return to the oven and bake for another 5–10 minutes.

Leave tarts to cool slightly before serving.

Makes 4 medium tarts

Panna Cotta Tartlets

Inspired by the Italian panna cotta desserts, this version sits in a shortcrust tart shell, so you can pop the whole tart in your mouth and enjoy!

Shortcrust pastry	1 quantity (see pg 140)
Milk	200 ml (6$^1/_2$ fl oz)
Double (heavy) cream	100 ml (3$^1/_3$ fl oz)
Sugar	2 Tbsp
Vanilla essence	1 tsp
Gelatine powder	1 Tbsp
Assorted berries	

Preheat oven to 180°C (350°F).

Roll pastry out on a floured surface to about 0.3-cm ($^1/_8$-in) thick.

Line the base and sides of 20–24 small, fluted tartlet tins with pastry and trim edges to neaten. Fill with beans, rice or baking weights and bake for 10 minutes or until golden brown. Remove weights and set tart shells aside to cool.

Mix milk and cream in a bowl, then whisk in sugar and vanilla essence. Place mixture over a pot of boiling water and continue whisking until mixture is slightly warm.

Dissolve gelatine powder in a small amount of warm water, then stir into milk mixture.

Spoon mixture into tartlet shells and refrigerate until set. Top with assorted berries and serve chilled.

Makes 20–24 tartlets

Passion Fruit Tarts

The unique flavour of passion fruit makes this tart a special treat. Save this recipe and serve it for those special occasions.

Shortcrust pastry	1 quantity (see pg 140)
Eggs	3
Egg yolk	1
Castor (superfine) sugar	150 g (5^1/$_3$ oz)
Double (heavy) cream	150 ml (5 fl oz)
Passion fruit coulis	200 ml (6^1/$_2$ fl oz)

Note: Passion fruit coulis is available from baking supply stores.

Preheat oven to 180°C (350°F).

Roll pastry out on a floured surface to about 0.3-cm (^{1}/$_8$-in) thick.

Line the base and sides of 4–6 medium tart tins with pastry and trim edges to neaten. Fill with beans, rice or baking weights and bake for 12–15 minutes or until golden brown. Remove weights and keep oven hot.

Meanwhile, whisk remaining ingredients together until sugar is dissolved. Pour into tart shells and return to the oven to bake until custard is set. Leave to cool before serving.

Garnish as desired.

Makes 4–6 medium tarts

shortcrust pastry

Lemon Tart

This brightly coloured tart is so pretty and delicious, it is ideal for serving at afternoon tea parties.

Sweet shortcrust pastry	1 quantity (see pg 140)
Lemon cordial	250 ml (8 fl oz / 1 cup)
Eggs	4
Whipping cream	300 ml (10 fl oz / 1$\frac{1}{4}$ cups)
Garnish	
Icing (confectioner's) sugar	for dusting
Lemons	2, cut into thin rounds and blanched

Preheat oven to 180°C (350°F).

Roll pastry out on a floured surface to about 0.3-cm ($\frac{1}{8}$-in) thick.

Line the base and sides of a 23-cm (9-in) loose-bottom tart pan with pastry and trim edges to neaten. Fill with beans, rice or baking weights and bake for 15 minutes. Remove weights and set tart shell aside to cool. Keep oven heated at 180°C (350°F).

Combine lemon cordial, eggs and cream in a mixing bowl and whisk until pale.

Pour mixture into tart shell and bake until filling is set. Takes about 20 minutes. Remove from oven and leave to cool before refrigerating until firm.

Arrange lemon slices on top of tart and dust with icing sugar. Serve with freshly whipped cream or ice cream if desired.

Makes one 23-cm (9-in) round tart

Lemon Curd Tartlets

Ensure that there are sufficient tartlets to go around! These tartlets are tart and tasty and will have your guests asking for more!

Shortcrust pastry	1 quantity (see pg 140)
Eggs	6
Sugar	200 g (7 oz)
Lemons	6, grated for zest and squeezed for juice

Note: If you are pressed for time, use ready-made tartlet shells available at baking supply stores.

Preheat oven to 180°C (350°F).

Roll pastry out on a floured surface to about 0.3-cm ($1/8$-in) thick.

Line the base and sides of 20–24 tartlet tins with pastry and trim edges to neaten. Fill with beans, rice or baking weights and bake for 10 minutes or until golden brown. Remove weights and set tart shells aside to cool.

Whisk eggs, sugar and lemon juice in a bowl set over a pot of boiling water until mixture is thick and coats the back of a wooden spoon. Leave to cool slightly.

Spoon lemon curd into tart shells. Refrigerate until chilled.

Blanch lemon zest in a pot of boiling water to remove any bitterness, then drain well. Top tartlets with lemon zest and serve chilled.

Makes 20–24 tartlets

Assorted Mini Fruit Tartlets

These dainty fruit tartlets satisfy sweet cravings without being too filling. Use a variety of fruit to add colour and excitement to your buffet table.

Shortcrust pastry	1 quantity (see pg 140)
Assorted fruit (raspberries, blueberries, cape gooseberries and strawberries)	
Custard	
Double (heavy) cream	200 ml ($6^{1}/_{2}$ fl oz)
Egg yolks	3
Castor (superfine) sugar	100 g ($3^{1}/_{2}$ oz)
Vanilla essence	1 Tbsp

Preheat oven to 180°C (350°F).

Roll pastry out on a floured surface to about 0.3-cm ($^{1}/_{8}$-in) thick.

Line the base and sides of 20–24 tartlet tins with pastry and trim edges to neaten. Fill with beans, rice or baking weights and bake for 10 minutes or until golden brown. Remove weights and set tart shells aside to cool.

Prepare custard. Beat cream, egg yolks, sugar and vanilla essence in a mixing bowl until mixture is light and creamy.

Spoon custard into cooled tartlet shells and top with fruit. Serve chilled.

Makes 20–24 tartlets

Baked Unagi Tarts

Grilled unagi is commonly used in Japanese cooking. It is traditionally believed to provide stamina, so enjoy this unagi tart anytime you need an energy boost!

Shortcrust pastry	1 quantity (see pg 140)
Grilled unagi	400 g (14$^{1}/_{3}$ oz)
Eggs	2
Double (heavy) cream	100 ml (3$^{1}/_{3}$ fl oz)
Salt	to taste
Ground black pepper	to taste
Spring onion (scallion)	1, green leaves cut into fine julienne and soaked in cold water

Note: Grilled unagi is available from Japanese supermarkets.

Preheat oven to 180°C (350°F).

Roll pastry out on a floured surface to about 0.3-cm ($^{1}/_{8}$-in) thick.

Line the base and sides of four 10-cm (4-in) oval tart tins with pastry and trim edges to neaten. Fill with beans, rice or baking weights and bake for 15 minutes. Remove weights and set tart shells aside to cool. Keep oven heated at 180°C (350°F).

Trim unagi to fit tart shells, then place into tart shells.

Beat eggs and cream together until well combined. Season with salt and pepper and pour over unagi. Bake for about 20 minutes or until egg is cooked and set.

Garnish with spring onion and serve.

Makes four 10-cm (4-in) oval tarts

Free-form Braised Leek Tart

Leek retains its flavour well, even after long periods of cooking. This tart can be prepared ahead of time and heated up just before serving.

Shortcrust pastry	1 quantity (see pg 140)
Olive oil	1 Tbsp
Red onions	2, peeled and chopped
Australian leek	500 g (1 lb 1^1/$_2$ oz), cut into 3–4-cm (1–1^1/$_2$-in) lengths
Thyme	1 sprig, leaves chopped
White wine	100 ml (3^1/$_3$ fl oz)
Vegetable stock	100 ml (3^1/$_3$ fl oz)
Parmesan cheese	55 g (2 oz), grated
Baking Cream Custard	
Double (heavy) cream	200 ml (6^1/$_2$ fl oz)
Eggs	4
Salt	^{1}/$_4$ tsp
Freshly cracked black pepper	^{1}/$_4$ tsp

Preheat oven to 180°C (350°F).

Roll pastry out on a floured surface to about 0.3-cm (^{1}/$_8$-in) thick. Cut into a large 16-cm (6^1/$_2$-in) square and place on a lined baking tray. Bring the edges of pastry up to form a square container. Fill with beans, rice or baking weights and bake for 15 minutes. Remove weights and set tart shell aside to cool.

Heat oil over low heat. Add onions, leek and thyme. Cover and cook over low heat until onions are soft.

Add wine and stock, and continue to simmer until leek is just tender. Leave to cool.

Prepare baking cream custard. Combine cream, eggs, salt and pepper in a mixing bowl and mix well.

Reheat oven to 180°C (350°).

Arrange leek in tart shell and pour baking cream custard over. Bake for about 20 minutes or until custard is set. Sprinkle with cheese before serving.

Makes 1 large square tart

Marinated Herring and Chive Cream Tarts

Marinated herring may be rather salty, but the cream works to balance the flavours perfectly.

Shortcrust pastry	1 quantity (see pg 140)
Salad greens	a small handful
Marinated sliced herring	4 small pieces
Chopped chives	1/2 Tbsp
Whipped cream	100 ml (3 1/3 fl oz)
Salt	to taste
Ground black pepper	to taste

Note: Marinated herring is available in jars from gourmet supermarkets.

Preheat oven to 180°C (350°F).

Roll pastry out on a floured surface to about 0.3-cm (1/8-in) thick.

Line the base and sides of four 8-cm (3-in) round tart tins with pastry and trim edges to neaten. Fill with beans, rice or baking weights and bake for 15 minutes. Remove weights and set tart shells aside to cool.

Arrange salad greens in each tart shell and top up with sliced herring.

Mix chopped chives with whipped cream and season to taste with salt and pepper. Spoon over herring and garnish as desired.

Makes four 8-cm (3-in) round tarts

Cherry Tomato Balsamic Tarts

There is no need to add anything else to this tart, as the natural taste of the tomatoes is brought out by gently cooking them.

Shortcrust pastry	1 quantity (see pg 140)
Olive oil	1 Tbsp
Cherry tomatoes (red and yellow)	300 g (11 oz)
Thyme	1 sprig, leaves chopped
Balsamic vinegar	2 Tbsp

Preheat oven to 180°C (350°F).

Roll pastry out on a floured surface to about 0.3-cm ($1/8$-in) thick.

Line the base and sides of two 11.5-cm ($4^1/_2$-in) round tart tins with pastry and trim edges to neaten. Fill with beans, rice or baking weights and bake for 15 minutes. Remove weights and set tart shells aside to cool.

Heat oil in a pan. Add tomatoes and thyme and cook briefly. Remove from heat and allow to cool slightly.

Arrange tomatoes in tart shells and drizzle with balsamic vinegar before serving warm.

Makes two 11.5-cm ($4^1/_2$-in) round tarts

Mushroom Ragout Tarts

Use your favourite fresh mushrooms or any mushrooms that are in season for this tart.

Shortcrust pastry	1 quantity (see pg 140)
Butter	1 tsp
Assorted fresh mushrooms	250 g (9 oz), cleaned and diced
Red onion	1, peeled and finely chopped
Salt	to taste
Ground black pepper	to taste
Spring onions (scallions)	2, chopped
Baking cream custard	100 ml ($3^1/_3$ fl oz) (see pg 30)

Note: For extra flavour, drizzle the tart with some white truffle oil just before serving.

Preheat oven to 180°C (350°F).

Roll pastry out on a floured surface to about 0.3-cm ($^1/_8$-in) thick.

Line the base and sides of four 8-cm (3-in) round tart tins with pastry and trim edges to neaten. Fill with beans, rice or baking weights and bake for 15 minutes. Remove weights and set tart shells aside to cool. Keep oven heated at 180°C (350°F).

Heat butter in a pan over low heat. Add mushrooms and onion. Cover pan and cook over low heat until onion is soft but not brown.

Season to taste with salt and pepper. Sprinkle half the chopped spring onions in and remove from heat.

Spoon mixture into tart shells and pour baking cream custard over. Return to the oven and bake for about 15 minutes or until custard is set.

Remove tarts from tins and garnish with remaining spring onions. Serve immediately.

Makes four 8-cm (3-in) round tarts

Salad Niçoise Tarts

You do not need to serve croutons with this salad, because it comes with its own crisp and fragrant shortcrust base!

Shortcrust pastry	1 quantity (see pg 140)
Olive oil	6 Tbsp
Tuna loin	250 g (9 oz)
White sesame seeds	4 Tbsp, toasted
Hard-boiled eggs	2, peeled and each cut into 4 quarters
Cherry tomatoes	4, each cut in half
Gherkins	4, thinly sliced
French beans	150 g (5$^1/_3$ oz), sliced and blanched
Green olives	6
Daikon cress	a small handful
Avruga or black caviar	4 Tbsp

Preheat oven to 180°C (350°F).

Roll pastry out on a floured surface to about 0.3-cm ($^1/_8$-in) thick.

Line the base and sides of two 11.5-cm (4$^1/_2$-in) round tart tins with pastry and trim edges to neaten. Fill with beans, rice or baking weights and bake for 15 minutes. Remove weights and set tart shells aside to cool.

While tart shells are baking, heat 2 Tbsp olive oil and sear tuna on all sides until lightly browned. Roll in toasted sesame seeds, then cut into 0.5-cm ($^1/_4$-in) thick slices.

Place tuna, eggs, tomatoes, gherkins, French beans, olives and daikon cress into a bowl and toss with olive oil. Place into tart shells and garnish with caviar.

Makes two 11.5-cm (4$^1/_2$-in) round tarts

Free-form Port Wine-caramelised Shallot Tart

The shallots give a very sweet finishing to this tart, which is further enhanced by the flavour of the wine.

Shortcrust pastry	1 quantity (see pg 140)
Olive oil	1 Tbsp
Shallots	300 g (11 oz), peeled
Thyme	1 sprig, leaves chopped
Butter	2 tsp
Sugar	1 tsp
Port wine	125 ml (4 fl oz / $1/2$ cup)
Red wine	100 ml ($3^{1}/_{3}$ fl oz)
Baking cream custard	200 ml ($6^{1}/_{2}$ fl oz) (see pg 30)

Note: Serve this tart with foie gras. The sweetness of the shallots goes beautifully with foie gras.

Preheat oven to 180°C (350°F).

Roll pastry out on a floured surface to about 0.3-cm ($1/8$-in) thick. Cut into a large rectangle, about 25 x 18-cm (10 x 7-in) and place on a baking tray lined with greaseproof paper.

Bring the edges of pastry up to form a large rectangular container. Fill with beans, rice or baking weights and bake for 15 minutes. Remove weights and set tart shells aside to cool. Keep oven heated at 180°C (350°F).

Heat olive oil over low heat and add shallots and thyme. Cover and cook until shallots are slightly soft, then add butter and cook for another 5 minutes.

Add sugar until caramelised. Add wine and simmer until liquid evaporates.

Spoon mixture into tart shell and pour custard over. Bake for about 20 minutes or until custard is set. Leave to cool before serving.

Makes 1 large rectangular tart

Tomato and Mozzarella Tart

An attractive-looking tart that belies how easy it is to do!

Shortcrust pastry	1 quantity (see pg 140)
Tomatoes	1, sliced
Mozzarella cheese	200 g (7 oz), sliced
Salad greens	a handful
Semi-dried tomatoes	as desired
Balsamic vinegar	for drizzling
Olive oil	for drizzling

Preheat oven to 180°C (350°F).

Roll pastry out on a floured surface to about 0.3-cm (1/8-in) thick. Cut into a large 16-cm (61/2-in) square and place on a baking tray lined with greaseproof paper.

Top pastry with tomato and cheese slices, then bake for about 25 minutes, or until pastry is golden brown and cheese is melted.

Place salad greens and semi-dried tomatoes on tart and drizzle with balsamic vinegar and olive oil. Serve immediately while cheese is still soft.

Makes one 16-cm (61/2-in) square tart

Smoked Salmon Tarts with Gherkins

Baking smoked salmon makes the taste even more intense, but the gherkins help balance out the flavour.

Shortcrust pastry	1 quantity (see pg 140)
Smoked salmon	200 g (7 oz)
Baking cream custard	100 ml (3$^{1}/_{3}$ fl oz)
Gherkins	2, small, sliced

Note: To reduce the saltiness of the smoked salmon, sprinkle some raw chopped onions over the salmon before adding the custard and baking.

Preheat oven to 180°C (350°F).

Roll pastry out on a floured surface to about 0.3-cm ($^{1}/_{8}$-in) thick.

Line the base and sides of four 8-cm (3-in) round tart tins with pastry and trim edges to neaten. Fill with beans, rice or baking weights and bake for 15 minutes. Remove weights and set tart shells aside to cool. Keep oven heated at 180°C (350°F).

Sliced smoked salmon and line base of tart shells. Pour baking cream custard over and bake for about 15 minutes or until custard is set.

Remove tarts from tins and arrange sliced gherkins on top before serving.

Makes four 8-cm (3-in) round tarts

Puff Pastry

Poached Red Wine Pear Tarts *49*

Caramelised Plum Tarts *50*

Banana Tarte Tatin *53*

Seared Scallop Layered Tarts with Mango Salsa *56*

Roast Pork Tartlets *57*

Asparagus and Fried Egg Tarts *58*

Braised Fennel Tarts with Orange Salad *61*

Grilled Capsicum Vol Au Vont *62*

Smoked Bratwurst Tarts with Sautéed Onions *65*

Artichoke Tarts with Olive Salsa *66*

Tandoori Salmon and Cucumber Yoghurt Tarts *69*

Smoked Turkey and Red Onion Jam Stacks *70*

Parma Ham, Apricot and Tomato Tarts *73*

Hoisin Chicken Tarts *74*

Poached Red Wine Pear Tarts

For perfect pairing of wine and dessert, use the same red wine you'll be serving to poach the pears.

Red wine	500 ml (16 fl oz / 2 cups)
Blackcurrant syrup	250 ml (8 fl oz / 1 cup)
Sugar	100 g (3^1/$_2$ oz)
Peckham pears	4
Ready-rolled puff pastry	1 square sheet

Preheat oven to 220°C (440°F).

Combine wine, blackcurrant syrup and sugar in a pot and bring to the boil.

Peel pears and poach in wine syrup until soft but not mushy. Takes 10–15 minutes.

Remove pears and slice thinly. Continue to simmer wine syrup over low heat until reduced and thick.

Using an 8-cm (3-in) round cutter, cut pastry into 4 rounds. Place on a baking tray and arrange pear slices on pastry.

Bake for about 20 minutes or until pastry is puffed and golden brown. Drizzle with reduced wine syrup if desired.

Makes four 8-cm (3-in) round tarts

Caramelised Plum Tarts

Plums are seasonal, so take advantage of them whenever they are in season to make this attractive dessert.

Butter	80 g (3 oz)
Sugar plums	8, halved, stone removed and cut into wedges
Sugar	100 g (3^1/$_2$ oz)
Ready-rolled puff pastry	1 square sheet
Icing (confectioner's) sugar	for dusting

Note: You may wish to brush the pastry with some egg wash before baking to give the tart an attractive glaze.

Preheat oven to 220°C (440°F).

Heat a pan over medium heat. Add butter, then plums and sugar. Stir until sugar melts and coats plums. Set aside to cool.

Cut pastry in half to get 2 rectangular sheets. Place on a baking tray.

Divide caramelised plums evenly and arrange on pastry sheets. Bake for 10–15 minutes or until pastry is puffed and golden brown.

Dust with icing sugar and serve immediately.

Makes 2 large tarts

Banana Tarte Tatin

Tarte Tatin is the name given to upside down tarts originating from France. This heavenly dessert is made with caramelised bananas.

Ready-rolled puff pastry	1 square sheet
Sugar	200 g (7 oz)
Water	1 Tbsp
Butter	100 g (3½ oz)
Bananas	6, medium, peeled and cut into 1.5-cm (1-in) thick rounds

Preheat oven to 220°C (440°F).

Using a 20-cm (8-in) round baking pan as a mould, cut out a round of pastry. Cover and keep refrigerated.

Place the baking pan on the stove over medium heat. Add sugar and water. Once sugar starts to caramelise, add butter, then bananas. Arrange bananas so bottom of pan is fully covered.

Place pastry on top of bananas and place pan in oven. Bake for about 25 minutes or until pastry is golden brown.

Remove pan from oven and turn tart out onto a serving dish. Serve immediately.

Makes one 20-cm (8-in) round tart

Seared Scallop Layered Tarts with Mango Salsa

This multi-tiered tart shell gives the usually flat tart added height.

Ready-rolled puff pastry	1 square sheet
Cooking oil	1/2 Tbsp
Scallops	4, large
Salt	to taste
Ground black pepper	to taste
Tobiko	1 tsp
Mango Salsa	
Ripe mango	1, peeled and diced
Red onion	1, peeled and finely chopped
Spring onion (scallion)	10 g (1/3 oz), finely chopped
Red chilli	1, seeded and finely chopped
Honey	1 tsp
Lemons	2, squeezed for juice

Prepare mango salsa. Combine all ingredients for salsa and mix well. Keep refrigerated until needed.

Preheat oven to 220°C (440°F).

Using a round cutter slightly larger than scallops, cut pastry into 8 rounds. Place on a baking tray.

Bake pastry rounds for about 10 minutes until pastry is puffed and golden brown. Remove from oven. Cut pastry rounds across in half, then stack 4 halves together to get 4 layered pastry shells.

Heat oil in a pan. Season scallops with salt and pepper to taste, then sear over high heat until colour changes and scallops are cooked.

Place scallops on top of pastry shells and top with mango salsa. Garnish with tobiko or as desired. Serve immediately.

Makes 4 small round tarts

Roast Pork Tartlets

The sweetness of the pineapple goes very well with the savoury roast pork. These make an excellent finger food.

Ready-rolled puff pastry	1 square sheet
Chinese-style roast pork	200 g (7 oz), cut into 24–30 strips, each about 1-cm ($1/2$-in) thick
Pineapple	100 g ($3^1/2$ oz)
Butter	1 Tbsp
Sugar	1 Tbsp

Preheat oven to 220°C (440°F).

Cut pastry into 24–30 small rectangles, slightly larger than roast pork strips.

Place a strip of roast pork on each pastry rectangle and bake for about 10 minutes until pastry is puffed and golden brown.

Cut pineapple into small strips the length of roast pork strips.

Heat a pan over medium heat and melt butter. Add pineapple and sugar and cook until sugar is melted and coats pineapple.

Place caramelised pineapple strips on top of roast pork. Serve immediately.

Makes 24–30 tartlets

Asparagus and Fried Egg Tarts

Serve this for breakfast for an excellent start to the day.

Ready-rolled puff pastry	1 square sheet
Asparagus	12 spears, peeled
Eggs	4, fried sunny-side up
Semi-dried tomatoes	150 g (5^1/$_3$ oz)
Olive oil	for drizzling
Salt	to taste
Ground black pepper	to taste

Preheat oven to 220°C (440°F).

Cut pastry in half, then halve each sheet again to get 4 triangles. Place pastry on a baking tray and arrange 3 asparagus spears on each triangle.

Bake for 12–15 minutes until pastry is puffed and golden brown.

Top with fried eggs, then bake for another 5 minutes.

Top with semi-dried tomatoes and drizzle with olive oil. Season with salt and pepper to taste. Serve immediately.

Makes 4 large tarts

Braised Fennel Tarts with Orange Salad

Braised fennel and orange are usually served as a salad with meat dishes. In this recipe, the salad is placed on a crisp puff pastry base, making it ideal as an appetiser or light lunch.

White wine	100 ml (3$^{1}/_{3}$ fl oz)
Vegetable stock	500 ml (16 fl oz / 2 cups)
Fennel bulbs	2
Ready-rolled puff pastry	1 square sheet
Orange	1
Olive oil	for drizzling

Preheat oven to 220°C (440°F).

Heat wine and stock over low heat and add fennel. Continue to cook over low heat until fennel is soft. Drain fennel and cut in half.

Cut pastry into 4 squares and place on a baking tray. Arrange a fennel half on each pastry square and bake for 12–15 minutes or until pastry is puffed and golden brown.

Meanwhile, grate zest from orange and blanch at least 3 times to remove any bitter taste. Set aside on paper towels to dry.

Cut orange into segments without the membrane.

Remove tarts from oven and top with orange zest and segments. Drizzle with olive oil and serve.

Makes 4 small tarts

Grilled Capsicum Vol Au Vont

Basically a salad made into a tart. Delightfully easy to put together yet so attractive.

Ready-rolled puff pastry	2 square sheets
Egg	1, well-beaten
Red, yellow and green capsicums (bell peppers)	300 g (11 oz), cored, seeded and sliced
Salt	to taste
Ground black pepper	to taste
Thyme	1 sprig, leaves chopped
Balsamic Reduction	
Balsamic vinegar	500 ml (16 fl oz / 2 cups)
Sugar	2 Tbsp

Preheat oven to 220°C (440°F).

Using an 8-cm (3-in) ring cutter, cut 8 rounds of puff pastry. Using a 6-cm (2½-in) ring cutter, cut a hole in the centre of 4 rounds and place each on top of remaining whole rounds, using some beaten egg to keep pastry in place when baking.

Brush top of pastry cases with remaining beaten egg, then place on a baking tray. Bake for 12–15 minutes until puffed and golden brown.

Prepare balsamic reduction. Bring balsamic vinegar and sugar to the boil in a small saucepan, then lower heat and simmer until reduced by two-thirds.

Season capsicums with salt, pepper and thyme. Grill to cook lightly, then set aside.

Arrange grilled capsicums in pastry or vol au vont cases. Drizzle with balsamic reduction and serve immediately.

Makes 4 medium tarts

Smoked Bratwurst Tarts with Sautéed Onions

Those who enjoy the traditional sausage roll will definitely love this version!

Ready-rolled puff pastry	1 square sheet
Smoked chicken bratwurst	450 g (1 lb), about 4 sausages
Olive oil	1 Tbsp
Red onions	125 g (4$^{1}/_{2}$ oz), peeled and sliced
Mustard Mayonnaise	
French mustard	1 Tbsp
Mayonnaise	100 ml (3$^{1}/_{3}$ fl oz)
Lemon	1, squeezed for juice

Preheat oven to 220°C (440°F).

Using an 8-cm (3-in) round cutter, cut 4 rounds of pastry. Place on a baking tray.

Cut each sausage on the diagonal into 4 pieces. Arrange on pastry rounds and bake for 10–12 minutes until pastry is light golden brown.

Meanwhile, heat oil in a pan and sauté onion until soft.

Top pastry with sautéed onions and bake for another 5 minutes.

While tarts are baking, combine ingredients for mustard mayonnaise. Serve tarts warm, drizzled with mustard mayonnaise.

Makes four 8-cm (3-in) round tarts

Artichoke Tarts with Olive Salsa

This Italian-inspired tart uses canned artichokes, making it a breeze to prepare!

Canned artichokes	1 can, about 385 g (14 oz), drained
Ready-rolled puff pastry	1 square sheet
Olives	100 g (3$^1/_2$ oz), finely chopped
Red onions	2, peeled and finely chopped
Olive oil	4 Tbsp

Preheat oven to 220°C (440°F).

Cut pastry in half to get 2 rectangles.

Cut each artichoke in half and arrange on puff pastry rectangles. Bake for about 25 minutes or until pastry is puffed and golden brown.

Toss chopped olives and onions with olive oil. Spoon over artichokes and serve immediately.

Makes 2 large tarts

Tandoori Salmon and Cucumber Yoghurt Tarts

Tandoori marinade is usually used for chicken, beef or lamb, but it also works beautifully with salmon.

Ready-rolled puff pastry	2 square sheets
Egg	1, beaten
Salmon fillet	300 g (11 oz), sliced
Tandoori marinade	55 g (2 oz)
Cucumber	1, cut into fine strips
Plain yoghurt	200 ml (6$^1/_2$ fl oz)
Salt	to taste
Ground black pepper	to taste
Ground cumin	$^1/_8$ tsp
Garnish	
Red capsicum (bell pepper)	$^1/_4$, cut into fine strips

Note: Tandoori marinade is available from the supermarkets.

Preheat oven to 220°C (350°F).

Cut each pastry sheet in half to get 4 rectangles. Leaving a 2.5-cm (1-in) border all around, cut out the centre portion of 2 puff pastry rectangles. Brush each frame with beaten egg and place on top of a remaining rectangle.

Place pastry on a baking tray and bake for 10–12 minutes until puffed and golden brown.

Rub salmon with tandoori marinade and set aside while pastry is baking.

Arrange salmon in hollow of pastry cases, then bake for another 10 minutes.

Combine cucumber and yoghurt, reserving some cucumber strips for garnish. Season yoghurt with salt, pepper and cumin.

Top tarts with cucumber yoghurt and garnish with capsicum and reserved cucumber strips before serving.

Makes 2 large tarts

Smoked Turkey and Red Onion Jam Stacks

This recipe offers a great way to make use of leftover turkey.

Ready-rolled puff pastry	1 square sheet
Olive oil	1 Tbsp
Red onions	300 g (11 oz), peeled and sliced
Red wine	100 ml ($3^{1}/_{3}$ fl oz)
Blackcurrant syrup	4 Tbsp
Bay leaf	1
Smoked turkey breast	200 g (7 oz), thinly sliced to fit pastry cases

Preheat oven to 220°C (440°F).

Using a 5-cm (2-in) round cutter, cut out 8 rounds from pastry sheet. Place on a baking tray.

Bake pastry for about 10 minutes until puffed and golden brown. Remove from oven. Cut pastry rounds horizontally into 2 to obtain 16 thin rounds, then stack 4 rounds together to form 4 layered pastry shells.

Heat oil and sauté onions until soft, then add wine, blackcurrant syrup and bay leaf. Cook over low heat, stirring, until mixture is thick, with a consistency like jam.

Place smoked turkey on pastry and top with onion jam. Garnish as desired and serve.

Makes four 5-cm (2-in) round tarts

Parma Ham, Apricot and Tomato Tarts

The sweetness of the apricots and juiciness of the tomatoes complement the flavour of the parma ham well. Try this recipe for a taste of something different.

Ready-rolled puff pastry	1 square sheet
Parma ham	125 g (4½ oz)
Dried apricots	85 g (3 oz), sliced
Cherry tomatoes	100 g (3½ oz), cut into wedges
Spring onion (scallion)	20 g (⅔ oz), finely chopped
Olive oil	for drizzling

Preheat oven to 220°C (440°F).

Cut pastry in half to get 2 rectangular sheets and place on a baking tray.

Bake pastry for 5 minutes, then remove and top with ham. Return to the oven and bake for another 5–7 minutes until pastry is light golden brown.

Top with apricots and tomatoes and bake for another 5 minutes.

Garnish with spring onion and drizzle with olive oil. Serve immediately.

Makes 2 large tarts

Hoisin Chicken Tarts

A pizza without cheese or an open sandwich on a puff pastry base. Whichever way you look at it, this tart makes a great snack at any time of the day.

Boneless chicken thigh	500 g (1 lb 1^1/$_2$ oz), cut into small pieces
Hoisin sauce	100 ml (3^1/$_3$ fl oz)
Salt	to taste
Ground black pepper	to taste
Ready-rolled puff pastry	1 square sheet
Salad greens	a handful

Preheat oven to 220°C (440°F).

Marinate chicken with hoisin sauce, salt and pepper.

Cut pastry in half, then cut each half into 2 triangles.

Divide chicken into 4 equal portions and place on pastry. Bake for about 25 minutes or until chicken is cooked and pastry is puffed and golden brown.

Garnish with salad greens and drizzle with hoisin sauce if desired.

Makes 4 medium tarts

Filo Pastry

Simple Baked Apple Tarts *78*

Crispy Tarts with Cranberry-Orange Relish *81*

Grilled Sarawak Pineapple Tarts *82*

Wok-fried Mushroom Ragout in Filo Cups *85*

Grilled Haloumi Cheese Stack *86*

Tuna Tartar in Filo Cones *88*

Caramelised Red Onion and Anchovy Tarts *89*

Crabmeat Filo Tart *93*

Foie Gras Mousse and Apricot Tarts *94*

Semi-dried Tomato Salsa Tarts *97*

Simple Baked Apple Tarts

Just as good as the traditional apple tart, but made with filo pastry rather than shortcrust pastry, for a dessert that is as tempting but lighter.

Filo (phyllo) pastry	6 sheets
Melted butter	for brushing pastry
Green apples	4
Sugar syrup	100 ml ($3^{1}/_{3}$ fl oz)
Icing (confectioner's) sugar	for dusting
Vanilla ice cream (optional)	

Note: These tarts can be made ahead of time and kept frozen without baking. Remove from the freezer and bake as needed.

Preheat oven to 180°C (350°F).

Place 1 sheet of filo pastry on a lined baking tray and brush with melted butter. Layer with another filo sheet and brush again with butter. Repeat with the third sheet of filo, then cut pastry into 2 rectangles. Repeat with remaining sheets of filo.

Slice apple with a mandoline or slice thinly with a sharp knife. Soak apple slices in sugar syrup for 10 minutes. Drain and pat dry with paper towels.

Arrange apple slices on pastry rectangles and fold edges of pastry up slightly around apples. Bake for about 10 minutes or until pastry is golden brown.

Dust lightly with icing sugar and serve with a scoop of vanilla ice cream if desired.

Makes 4 medium tarts

Crispy Tarts with Cranberry-Orange Relish

Cranberries and oranges blended together into a purée make a refreshing filling for this tart.

Wanton skins	4 round sheets
Cooking oil	for deep-frying
Fresh cranberries	200 g (7 oz)
Oranges	2, peeled and segmented
Sugar	to taste

Note: Prepare the filling ahead of time and keep refrigerated. This will help the flavours develop.

Press each wanton sheet into a small round heatproof mould or any small mould of choice.

Heat oil for deep-frying and lower moulds into hot oil. Deep-fry until golden brown. Remove and drain well.

Blend cranberries and orange segments together into a purée. Stir in sugar to taste.

Spoon filling into tart shells just before serving.

Makes 4 small tarts

Grilled Sarawak Pineapple Tarts

Sarawak pineapples are known for their sweet taste and grilling brings out their full flavour.

Sarawak pineapple	1/2, medium, peeled
Filo (phyllo) pastry	9 sheets
Melted butter	for brushing pastry
Icing (confectioner's) sugar	for dusting

Note: Use honey pineapples if Sarawak pineapples are not available. You may also use canned pinapple if preferred.

Preheat oven to 180°C (350°F).

Cut pineapple into wedges. Remove core and cut wedges into 1-cm (1/2-in) thick slices. Lightly grill pineapple.

Place 1 sheet of filo pastry on a lined baking tray and brush with melted butter. Layer with another filo sheet and brush again with butter. Repeat with the third sheet of filo, then cut pastry into 4 squares. Lay pastry on a baking sheet. Repeat with remaining filo sheets.

Arrange pineapple slices on pastry and bake for about 10 minutes or until pastry is golden brown.

Dust lightly with icing sugar and serve immediately.

Makes 12 small tarts

Wok-fried Mushroom Ragout in Filo Cups

Definitely a mushroom lover's treat! Use your favourite fresh mushrooms or any mushroom that is in season.

Filo (phyllo) pastry	3 sheets
Melted butter	for brushing pastry
Cooking oil	1 Tbsp
Red onion	1, peeled and chopped
Assorted fresh mushrooms (button, shiitake, oyster etc.)	200 g (7 oz)
Salt	to taste
Ground black pepper	to taste
Balsamic reduction	2 Tbsp (see pg 62)
Enoki mushrooms	a small handful

Preheat oven to 180°C (350°F).

Place 1 sheet of filo pastry on a lined baking tray and brush with melted butter. Layer with another filo sheet and repeat to brush with butter. Repeat with the third sheet of filo.

Cut filo into 4 squares, then place onto 4 overturned medium moulds. Bake for 10 minutes or until pastry is golden brown. Remove from oven and leave to cool.

Meanwhile, heat oil in a pan and fry onion until soft, then add mushrooms. Season to taste with salt and pepper and toss to mix.

Drizzle balsamic reduction over just before removing from heat. Spoon ragout into filo cups and garnish with enoki mushrooms.

Makes 4 small tarts

Grilled Haloumi Cheese Stack

Prepare the filo pastry ahead of time and arrange it when ready to serve. This tart is ideal when you are pressed for time when planning for a party.

Filo (phyllo) pastry	3 sheets
Melted butter	for brushing pastry
Haloumi cheese	250 g (9 oz), cut into long strips
Semi-dried tomatoes	55 g (2 oz)
Stuffed olives	55 g (2 oz)
Olive oil	for drizzling

Preheat oven to 180°C (350°F).

Place 1 sheet of filo pastry on a lined baking tray and brush with melted butter. Layer with another filo sheet and brush again with butter. Repeat with the third sheet of filo, then cut pastry into 3 rectangular strips. Bake for about 10 minutes or until golden brown.

Stack baked filo rectangles, then top with grilled haloumi cheese, tomatoes and olives. Drizzle with olive oil and serve immediately.

Makes 1 medium tart

Tuna Tartar in Filo Cones

These make great starters or finger foods. They are not only pleasing to the eye, but also a wonderful treat for the taste buds!

Filo (phyllo) pastry	3 sheets
Melted butter	for brushing pastry
Sashimi-grade tuna	150 g (5$^{1}/_{3}$ oz), finely diced
Red onion	1, peeled and finely diced
Spring onion (scallion)	1, finely chopped
Semi-dried tomatoes	4, finely chopped
Pickled ginger	3 slices, finely chopped
Tabasco sauce	1 Tbsp
Salt	to taste
Ground black pepper	to taste
Lime	1, squeezed for juice

Preheat oven to 180°C (350°F).

Place 1 sheet of filo pastry on a lined baking tray and brush with melted butter. Layer with another filo sheet and repeat to brush with butter. Repeat with the third sheet of filo.

Cut filo into 4 squares, then place onto 4 cone-shaped moulds. Bake for 10 minutes or until pastry is golden brown. Remove from oven and leave to cool.

Combine tuna, onion, spring onion, semi-dried tomatoes, pickled ginger and Tabasco sauce. Season with salt, pepper and lime juice. Spoon mixture into cones and serve immediately.

Makes 4 small tarts

Caramelised Red Onion and Anchovy Tarts

The onions are cooked over low heat to ensure that they take on a soft, melting texture and become sweet and full of flavour.

Filo (phyllo) pastry	3 sheets
Melted butter	for brushing pastry
Cooking oil	1 Tbsp
Red onions	300 g (11 oz), peeled and sliced
Canned anchovy fillets	85 g (3 oz)
Daikon sprouts	a small handful

Preheat oven to 180°C (350°F).

Place 1 sheet of filo pastry on a lined baking tray and brush with melted butter. Layer with another filo sheet and repeat to brush with butter. Repeat with the third sheet of filo.

Cut filo into 4 squares, then place onto 4 overturned medium moulds. Bake for 10 minutes or until pastry is golden brown. Remove from oven and leave to cool.

Heat oil in a pan over low heat and add onions. Continue cooking over low heat until onions are soft and translucent. Leave to cool.

Spoon onions into filo cups and top with anchovies just before serving. Garnish with daikon sprouts and serve immediately.

Makes 4 small tarts

Photo on pp 90–91

Crabmeat Filo Tart

This savoury tart is easily put together using canned crabmeat, doing away with the hassle of cooking the crabs and picking the meat from the shells.

Filo (phyllo) pastry	3 sheets
Melted butter	for brushing pastry
Canned crabmeat	400 g (14$\frac{1}{3}$ oz), drained
Basil leaves	5, finely sliced
Red onions	2, peeled and finely chopped
Spring onion (scallion)	1, finely chopped
Japanese mayonnaise	3 Tbsp
Salt	to taste
Ground white pepper	to taste
Lumpfish roe	to garnish
Semi-dried tomatoes	to garnish

Preheat oven to 180°C (350°F).

Place 1 sheet of filo pastry on a lined baking tray and brush with melted butter. Layer with another filo sheet and repeat to brush with butter. Repeat with the third sheet of filo.

Place filo in a loaf tin and bake for about 10 minutes or until golden brown.

Combine crabmeat with basil, onions, spring onion and mayonnaise. Mix well. Season to taste with salt and pepper.

Spoon mixture into filo tart shell just before serving. Garnish with roe and semi-dried tomatoes and serve immediately.

Makes 1 large tart

Foie Gras Mousse and Apricot Tarts

A simple yet sophisticated gourmet tart that will be the highlight of any party.

Filo (phyllo) pastry	3 sheets
Melted butter	for brushing pastry
Foie gras mousse	1 can, 320 g (11$^{2}/_{3}$ oz)
Apricot Jam	
Canned apricots	150 g (5$^{1}/_{3}$ oz), chopped
Red onions	2, peeled and finely chopped
White wine vinegar	100 ml (3$^{1}/_{3}$ fl oz)

Note: Canned foie gras mousse is available from gourmet supermarkets. Alternatively, pan-fry foie gras and use in place of mousse.

Preheat oven to 180°C (350°F).

Place 1 sheet of filo pastry on a lined baking tray and brush with melted butter. Layer with another filo sheet and brush again with butter. Repeat with the third sheet of filo, then using an 8-cm (3-in) fluted ring cutter, cut out 4 rounds.

Bake pastry rounds for about 10 minutes or until golden brown. Set aside to cool.

Combine apricots, onions and vinegar in a small pot. Cook over low heat, stirring constantly to prevent burning, until mixture is thick, with a consistency like marmalade.

Using a 4-cm (1$^{1}/_{2}$-in) round ring cutter, cut mousse into 4 rounds and place on pastry rounds. Top with apricot jam and garnish as desired. Serve immediately.

Makes four 8-cm (3-in) round tarts

Semi-dried Tomato Salsa Tarts

All the flavours of the Mediterranean in a light and crisp tart shell made of spring roll skin.

Spring roll skin	1 large square sheet
Cooking oil	for deep-frying
Store-bought semi-dried tomato salsa	100 g (3^1/$_2$ oz), finely chopped
Red onion	1, peeled and finely chopped
Spring onion (scallion)	1, finely chopped

Note: The liquid from the salsa will soften the tart shell if left too long. Spoon the salsa into the shells just before serving.

Cut spring roll skin into 4 squares. Press each sheet into a small square heatproof mould or any small mould of choice.

Heat oil for deep-frying and lower moulds into hot oil. Deep-fry spring roll skins until golden brown. Remove and drain well.

Toss tomato salsa, onion and spring onion together and mix well. Spoon into shells and serve immediately.

Makes 4 small tarts

Vegetable and other Bases

Chocolate Filled Poached Apricots *100*

Prawn Salad in Egg White Shells *103*

Egg and Caviar in New Potato Shells *104*

Olives Stuffed in Japanese Cucumber Cups *107*

Tomato and Pickled Ginger Salsa in
Cherry Tomato Shells *108*

Wild Mushroom Ragout in Courgette Shells *111*

Crabmeat and Mango in Avocado Boats *112*

Scallop Ragout in Button Mushroom Caps *115*

Feta Cheese in Watermelon Squares *116*

Goat Cheese in Roma Tomato Shells *119*

Chocolate Filled Poached Apricots

Chocolate in apricot cups. These simple tarts are strikingly attractive yet simply delicious!

Dark chocolate	300 g (11 oz), broken into pieces
Double (heavy) cream	300 ml (10 fl oz / 1^1/$_4$ cups)
Canned apricot halves	10

Place chocolate and cream into a dry bowl placed over a pot of boiling water. Do not let water get into chocolate. Stir until chocolate is melted. Remove chocolate from heat and leave to cool slightly.

When chocolate is cool, spoon into apricot halves and allow to set. Garnish as desired and serve.

Makes 10 small tarts

Prawn Salad in Egg White Shells

These tarts are great when you want something that is light on the taste buds, yet substantial enough to satisfy a craving.

Hard-boiled eggs	4, small, peeled
Prawns (shrimps)	350 g (12 oz), medium
Red onions	2, peeled and finely chopped
Spring onion (scallion)	20 g ($2/3$ oz), finely chopped
Mayonnaise	2 Tbsp
Salt	to taste
Ground black pepper	to taste

Note: You may serve these tarts in spoons with a flat base such as Chinese spoons, so the eggs will stand on their own without toppling over.

Cut hard-boiled eggs in half lengthwise, then remove yolks. Reserve yolks for use in another recipe.

Steam prawns until colour changes and prawns are cooked. Peel and set 8 prawns aside. Chop remaining prawns finely.

Mix chopped prawns with onions, spring onion and mayonnaise. Season with salt and pepper to taste.

Spoon mixture into egg white shells and top with whole cooked prawns. Garnish as desired and serve.

Makes 8 small tarts

Egg and Caviar in New Potato Shells

The hard-boiled egg filling does not require seasoning as the caviar provides all the necessary flavour.

New potatoes	8, boiled until tender
Hard-boiled eggs	4, peeled and finely chopped
Black caviar	as desired

Cut potatoes in half, then using a melon baller, scoop out some flesh from centre of potatoes. Be careful not to cut through potatoes.

Trim base of potato halves so potatoes can stand on their own.

Spoon chopped hard-boiled eggs into potatoes and garnish with caviar.

Makes 16 small tarts

Olives Stuffed in Japanese Cucumber Cups

Another simple dish that is simply bursting with flavour.

Japanese cucumbers	3, each cut into 5–6 rounds, about 2.5-cm (1-in) thick	Use a melon baller to scoop out the centre of each cucumber round.
Tomatoes	2, large	Cut a small 'x' on the base of tomatoes and blanch in boiling water. Drain and leave to cool slightly before peeling tomatoes. Cut peeled tomatoes in half, then remove seeds and dice tomatoes finely.
Green olives	200 g (7 oz), finely chopped	
Red onion	1, peeled and finely chopped	Combine olives, onion and tomatoes. Mix well, then spoon into cucumber cups. Garnish as desired and serve.

Makes 15–18 small tarts

Tomato and Pickled Ginger Salsa in Cherry Tomato Shells

These cute little tarts can be prepared in a jiffy!

Cherry tomatoes	12, large
Tomatoes	2, large
Pickled ginger	20 g ($2/3$ oz), finely chopped
Spring onion (scallion)	20 g ($2/3$ oz), finely chopped
Red onion	20 g ($2/3$ oz), peeled and finely chopped
Salt	to taste
Ground black pepper	to taste
Lime	1, squeezed for juice

Cut caps off cherry tomatoes and scoop out seeds. Trim base of cherry tomatoes so they can stand on their own. Set aside.

Cut a small 'x' on the base of tomatoes and blanch in boiling water. Drain and leave to cool slightly before peeling tomatoes. Cut peeled tomatoes in half, then remove seeds and dice tomatoes finely.

Mix diced tomatoes with pickled ginger, spring onion and onion. Season to taste with salt, pepper and lime juice.

Spoon mixture into cherry tomatoes, garnish as desired and serve.

Makes 12 small tarts

Wild Mushroom Ragout in Courgette Shells

A mushroom lover's delight! This vegetable tart is aromatic and full of the earthy flavour of fresh mushrooms.

Yellow courgettes (zucchinis)	3
Butter	1 Tbsp
Red onions	2, peeled and finely chopped
Assorted mushrooms	250 g (9 oz), finely chopped
Salt	to taste
Ground black pepper	to taste
Double (heavy) cream	100 ml ($3^1/_3$ fl oz)
Spring onions (scallions)	45 g ($1^1/_2$ oz), finely chopped

Note: Choose courgettes that are similar in size, and of an even circumference from stalk to base, so the tarts look more uniform when they are served.

Using a carving tool, make shallow grooves on the skin of courgettes at regular intervals to create a pattern, if desired. Cut ends off courgettes, then cut each courgette into 5–6 rounds, about 2.5-cm (1-in) thick.

Using a melon baller, scoop out the centre of each courgette round to create a depression.

Heat a pot of water and blanch courgettes. Drain and plunge immediately into ice water. Drain and pat dry with paper towels.

Heat butter in a pan over low heat and add onion. Cover and cook over low heat until softened, then add mushrooms. When mushrooms are softened, season with salt and pepper. Stir in cream and spring onion. Mix well.

Leave mixture to cool slightly, before spooning into courgette shells. Garnish and serve.

Makes 15–18 small tarts

Crabmeat and Mango in Avocado Boats

The rich creaminess of the avocado makes this a filling but extremely satisfying appetiser or snack.

Ripe avocados	2
Lemon juice	for soaking
Crabmeat	100 g (3$\frac{1}{2}$ oz)
Ripe mango flesh	100 g (3$\frac{1}{2}$ oz), finely diced
Red onions	2, peeled and finely diced
Spring onions (scallions)	20 g ($\frac{2}{3}$ oz), chopped
Salt	to taste
Ground black pepper	to taste
Lemon	1, squeezed for juice

Note: To test an avocado for ripeness, place it in the palm of your hand and squeeze gently. A ripe avocado will yield to the pressure.

Cut through avocados lengthwise until you reach the pit. Cut avocados around pit, then twist to separate the halves. Remove the pit, then insert a spoon between the skin and flesh and separate them carefully so avocado is not bruised.

Soak avocados in lemon juice to prevent oxidization.

Combine crabmeat, mango, red onions and spring onions. Season with salt, pepper and juice of 1 lemon.

Drain avocado halves. Spoon mixture into avocado halves. Garnish as desired and serve.

Serves 4

Scallop Ragout in Button Mushroom Caps

Button mushrooms make great tart shells. They are easy-to-prepare and will not crack or break as pastry shells would, if you are not careful!

Button mushrooms	4, large, stalks removed
Salt	to taste
Ground black pepper	to taste
Cooking oil	1 Tbsp
Scallops	125 g ($4^{1}/_{2}$ oz), poached to cook
Red onion	1, peeled and finely chopped
Spring onion (scallion)	20 g ($^{2}/_{3}$ oz), finely chopped
Red chilli	1, seeded and finely diced
Lime	1, squeezed for juice
Tobiko	4 tsp

Season mushrooms with salt and pepper.

Heat oil in a wok and add mushrooms. Stir-fry for about 3 minutes, then remove from heat and leave to cool.

Dice poached scallops and combine with onion, spring onion, chilli and lime juice. Season to taste with salt and pepper.

Spoon mixture into button mushroom caps and garnish with tobiko.

Makes 4 small tarts

Note: Choose button mushrooms of a similar size for a visually pleasing presentation.

Feta Cheese in Watermelon Squares

Inspired by the Greek summer salad of watermelon and feta cheese, this tart is ideal for serving between courses to refresh and cleanse the palate.

Red watermelon	½, small, cut into 8 cubes, each about 4-cm (1½-in)
Feta cheese	200 g (7 oz), cut into small cubes
Coriander Pesto	
Coriander leaves (cilantro)	100 g (3½ oz)
Peanuts	20 g (⅔ oz), roasted
Garlic	2 cloves, peeled
Palm sugar	3 Tbsp
Olive oil	100 ml (3⅓ fl oz)
Salt	to taste
Ground black pepper	to taste

Use a melon baller to scoop out the centre portion of each watermelon cube.

Place coriander leaves, peanuts, garlic, palm sugar and olive oil in a blender (food processor) and blend into a fine purée. Season to taste with salt and pepper.

Fill watermelon cubes with feta cheese, then top with pesto. Serve immediately.

Makes 8 small tarts

Goat Cheese in Roma Tomato Shells

Warm, baked tomato with melted cheese and a sweet apricot topping. Be prepared to provide second and even third helpings!

Roma (plum) tomatoes	4
Goat cheese	200 g (7 oz)
Baking cream custard	200 ml (6$^1/_2$ fl oz) (see pg 30)
Apricot jam (see pg 94)	

Preheat oven to 180°C (350°F).

Cut tomatoes across in half, then scoop out seeds. Slice off a small portion of the rounded base of tomato halves so they can sit on the baking tray.

Divide cheese into 8 equal portions and stuff into tomato shells.

Spoon baking cream custard over cheese and bake for about 15 minutes or until custard is set.

Top with apricot jam, garnish as desired and serve immediately.

Makes 8 small tarts

Chocolate and Biscuit Bases

Dark Chocolate Tarts *122*

Chocolate Cornflake Tarts with Kiwi Fruit *125*

Lime Mascarpone Tarts *126*

Dark Cherry Chocolate Tarts *129*

Avocado Purée Biscuit Tarts *130*

Strawberry Chocolate Tarts *133*

White Chocolate Mousse Tarts *134*

Hazelnut Praline Chocolate Tarts *137*

Dark Chocolate Tarts

Every chocolate lover's dream—the ultimate chocolate tart! Dark chocolate in a dark chocolate shell, topped with white chocolate shavings.

Dark chocolate tart shells	**4, medium (see pg 142)**
Dark chocolate	**250 g (9 oz)**
Double (heavy) cream	**250 ml (8 fl oz / 1 cup)**
White chocolate shavings	**as desired**

Prepare chocolate tart shells.

Place dark chocolate and cream into a dry bowl over a pot of boiling water. Do not let water get into chocolate. Stir until chocolate is melted. Remove chocolate from heat and leave to cool slightly.

When chocolate is cool, spoon into tart shells and allow to set. Top with white chocolate shavings and serve.

Makes 4 medium tarts

Chocolate Cornflake Tarts with Kiwi Fruit

Chocolate-coated cornflakes... a treat in itself! Here, it is a tart base for sweet kiwi fruit.

Dark chocolate	200 g (7 oz), broken into small pieces
Cornflakes	200 g (7 oz)
Double (heavy) cream	100 ml ($3^{1}/_{3}$ fl oz)
Kiwi fruit	4, peeled and cut into wedges

Melt half the dark chocolate in a small bowl over boiling water. Do not let water get into the chocolate.

Add cornflakes to melted chocolate and stir to coat well. Divide into 4 portions and spoon onto a sheet of greaseproof paper to form rough round shapes. Leave chocolate to cool and set.

Melt remaining dark chocolate with cream. Leave to cool and harden. Divide into 4 equal portions. Place each portion onto a cornflake tart base and top with wedges of kiwi fruit. Serve.

Makes 4 medium tarts

Lime Mascarpone Tarts

This tart has just a teeny bit of tartness to it to make it so delectable. With a sweet biscuit base, it is a non-baked cheesecake masquerading as a tart.

Sweet biscuit tart shells	4, medium (see pg 142)
Egg yolks	8
Lime juice	100 ml ($3^{1}/_{3}$ fl oz)
Castor (superfine) sugar	250 g (9 oz)
Butter	250 g (9 oz), softened at room temperature
Mascarpone	150 g ($5^{1}/_{3}$ oz)

Prepare biscuit tart shells.

Combine egg yolks, lime juice and sugar in a small mixing bowl set over a pot of boiling water. Beat until mixture is thick.

Continue beating while adding butter. Beat until mixture is thick and glossy. Leave mixture to cool, then fold in mascarpone.

Spoon mixture into tart shells. Garnish as desired and serve.

Makes 4 medium tarts

Dark Cherry Chocolate Tarts

Juicy, sweet, dark cherries embedded in a light, vanilla-flavoured custard, set in a dark chocolate shell. This is a dessert that has to be eaten with hands, so nothing is wasted!

Dark chocolate tart shells	4, medium (see pg 142)	
Custard	180 ml (6 fl oz / ¾ cup) (see pg 26)	
Pitted dark cherries	250 g (9 oz)	
Roasted peanuts	1 Tbsp, crushed	
Icing (confectioner's) sugar	for dusting	

Prepare chocolate tart shells.

Prepare custard.

Spoon custard into tart shells and arrange cherries on top. Sprinkle crushed peanuts over and dust with icing sugar before serving.

Makes 4 medium tarts

Avocado Purée Biscuit Tarts

Avocado purée is rich and creamy, not unlike ice cream. Served with a sweet biscuit base, it makes a wonderful treat.

Sweet biscuit tart shells	4, medium (see pg 142)
Avocados	2
Lemons	2, squeezed for juice
Sugar	1 Tbsp

Cut through avocados lengthwise until you reach the pit. Cut avocados around pit, then twist to separate the halves. Remove the pit, then insert a spoon between the skin and flesh and separate them.

Place avocados in a blender (food processor) with $1/2$ Tbsp water and blend into a smooth purée. Add more water as necessary to help blender blades move.

Add lemon juice and sugar, and blend again into a smooth purée. Spoon puree into tart shells and serve.

Makes 4 medium tarts

Strawberry Chocolate Tarts

This recipe was inspired by the classic dessert favourite of dark chocolate-coated strawberries—simple, yet irresistible!

Dark chocolate tart shells	4, medium (see pg 142)
Custard	180 ml (6 fl oz / ¾ cup) (see pg 26)
Strawberries	4, large, cleaned and hulled and cut into wedges
Icing (confectioner's) sugar	for dusting

Prepare tart shells.

Prepare custard.

Spoon custard into tart shells and arrange cut strawberries on top. Dust with icing sugar and garnish as desired. Serve.

Makes 4 medium tarts

White Chocolate Mousse Tarts

This glamorous dessert is sure to impress your guests. It requires some patience to prepare, but the end result is definitely worth it!

Dark chocolate tart shells	**10, medium (see pg 142)**
White chocolate	**200 g (7 oz), broken into small pieces**
Whipping cream	**200 ml (6^1/$_2$ fl oz)**
Raspberries	**10**

Prepare tart shells.

Place white chocolate and cream into a dry bowl set over a pot of boiling water. Do not let water get into chocolate. Stir until chocolate melts. Remove chocolate from heat and leave to cool.

Whip cream until soft peaks form.

Fold cream into cooled chocolate, then spoon into tart shells and leave to set. Garnish with raspberries and serve.

Makes 10 medium tarts

Hazelnut Chocolate Praline Tarts

This recipe is specially for those who prefer white chocolate.

White chocolate tart shells	4, medium (see pg 142)
Whipping cream	150 ml (5 fl oz), whipped
Hazelnut chocolate praline paste	150 g (5$^1/_3$ oz)

Note: Hazelnut chocolate praline paste is available at baking supply stores.

Prepare tart shells.

Whip cream until soft peaks form. Fold praline paste into cream.

Spoon paste into tart shells and leave to set. Garnish as desired and serve.

Makes 4 medium tarts

Basic Recipes

Puff Pastry

This recipe is only for those who truly enjoy making their own puff pastry dough. For those who prefer to do away with the hassle and the possibility of the dough not working out, ready-made puff pastry is available from the frozen section of supermarkets as ready-rolled sheets or in blocks. If making your own puff pastry, ensure the dough is well chilled before working with it. Insufficiently chilled dough will become greasy and tough when baked.

Plain (all-purpose) flour	225 g (8 oz)
Salt	1/8 tsp
Butter	180 g (6 1/2 oz), cut into cubes
Cold water	150 ml (5 fl oz)

Sift flour and salt into a mixing bowl. Using the tips of your fingers, rub 30 g (1 oz) butter into flour, then stir in just enough water to make a soft dough. Wrap dough in cling film and refrigerate for 20 minutes.

Place remaining butter between 2 sheets of greaseproof paper and roll it out into a flat rectangular sheet.

Roll chilled dough out into a sheet of similar size.

Place butter sheet on dough sheet and refrigerate for 10 minutes. Remove from refrigerator and roll dough and butter out, making it 3 times its original length.

Fold dough into thirds, then roll out again. Repeat this step for at least another 5 times before refrigerating for 30 minutes before using.

Shortcrust Pastry

Plain (all-purpose) flour	275 g (10 oz)
Salt	1/8 **tsp**
Cold butter	120 g (4^1/$_2$ oz), cut into cubes
Cold water	3 Tbsp

Place flour and salt in a blender (food processor). Pulse to mix well, then add butter and pulse again until mixture resembles fine breadcrumbs.

With motor running, add water to combine dough.

Remove dough from blender and wrap with cling film. Refrigerate for at least 1 hour or until firm before using.

Makes enough pastry for 1 large tart, 4 medium tarts or 12–24 small tarts.

Sweet Shortcrust Pastry

Cold butter	225 g (8 oz), cut into cubes
Icing (confectioner's) sugar	100 g (3^1/$_2$ oz)
Plain (all-purpose) flour	375 g (13^1/$_2$ oz)
Egg	1
Egg yolk	1, lightly beaten

Place butter, sugar and flour in a blender (food processor) and pulse until mixture resembles fine breadcrumbs.

With motor running, add egg and egg yolk to combine dough.

Remove dough from blender and wrap with cling film. Refrigerate for at least 1 hour or until firm before using.

Makes enough pastry for 1 large tart, 4 medium tarts or 12–24 small tarts.

Left: The mixture should resemble fine breadcrumbs.

Right: Weigh the pastry down with beans or baking weights so the crust does not rise during baking.

Tips on Working with Shortcrust Pastry

To get a light, crisp crust

Always use butter that has been sufficiently chilled. Softened butter will cause the crust to be greasy and hence lose its crisp texture.

Use a blender (food processor), if possible, when making shortcrust pastry. If using your hands in place of a blender, they should be cold to avoid melting the butter. Cool hands down by dipping into cold water, then dry hands well before touching dough.

Work on a cool surface to avoid melting the butter.

Do not overwork the dough. Stop kneading as soon as the pastry is formed.

When adding cold water to the butter and flour mixture, add a little at a time and mix gently. Do not add or mix more than necessary.

To avoid a soggy crust

When using a moist filling, always bake the crust sufficiently before adding the filling. This is known as "blind baking".

To get a golden brown crust

Do not underbake the crust. Ovens may heat and cook food differently, so watch that the crust is sufficiently brown before removing from the oven, even if this means exceeding the baking time specified in the recipe.

If the edges of the crust start to brown too quickly (before the base of the crust browns), cover (only the edges) with aluminium foil and continue baking until the crust is light golden brown.

Chocolate Tart shells

Chocolate (dark or white)	300 g (11 oz), broken into pieces

Place 200 g (7 oz) chocolate into a dry bowl set over a pot of boiling water. Do not let water get into chocolate. Stir until chocolate melts.

Remove from heat, then add remaining chocolate to cool the mixture to the right temperature. This is known as tempering the chocolate. Stir until mixture is smooth and glossy.

Spoon chocolate into a clean, dry mould and tilt mould around so chocolate coats the inside of mould. Pour excess chocolate back into bowl of tempered chocolate. Place mould upside down on a wire rack with a tray underneath to catch any drip. Leave chocolate to set. Repeat to make desired number of tart shells.

Knock the mould gently on a tabletop to remove set chocolate tart shell.

Makes 1 large tart, 4 medium tarts or 12–20 small tarts.

Sweet Biscuit Base

This biscuit base is so easy to make. Use your favourite biscuits and experiment with plain or chocolate biscuits to add variety!

Biscuits (grahams, oreos or digestives)	750 g (1 lb 11 oz)
Butter	250 g (9 oz), melted

Place biscuits in a plastic bag and crush well until biscuits are all broken up and crumbly. Pour into a mixing bowl and mix well with melted butter.

Spoon mixture into baking mould(s). Press well into base and sides of mould(s), then refrigerate for at least 30 minutes before using.

Makes 1 large tart, 4 medium tarts or 12–20 small tarts.

Weights and Measures

Quantities for this book are given in Metric and American (spoon and cup) measures. Standard spoon and cup measurements used are: 1 tsp = 5 ml, 1 Tbsp = 15 ml, 1 cup = 250 ml. All measures are level unless otherwise stated.

LIQUID AND VOLUME MEASURES

Metric	Imperial	American
5 ml	1/6 fl oz	1 teaspoon
10 ml	1/3 fl oz	1 dessertspoon
15 ml	1/2 fl oz	1 tablespoon
60 ml	2 fl oz	1/4 cup (4 tablespoons)
85 ml	2 1/2 fl oz	1/3 cup
90 ml	3 fl oz	3/8 cup (6 tablespoons)
125 ml	4 fl oz	1/2 cup
180 ml	6 fl oz	3/4 cup
250 ml	8 fl oz	1 cup
300 ml	10 fl oz (1/2 pint)	1 1/4 cups
375 ml	12 fl oz	1 1/2 cups
435 ml	14 fl oz	1 3/4 cups
500 ml	16 fl oz	2 cups
625 ml	20 fl oz (1 pint)	2 1/2 cups
750 ml	24 fl oz (1 1/5 pints)	3 cups
1 litre	32 fl oz (1 3/5 pints)	4 cups
1.25 litres	40 fl oz (2 pints)	5 cups
1.5 litres	48 fl oz (2 2/5 pints)	6 cups
2.5 litres	80 fl oz (4 pints)	10 cups

OVEN TEMPERATURE

	°C	°F	Gas Regulo
Very slow	120	250	1
Slow	150	300	2
Moderately slow	160	325	3
Moderate	180	350	4
Moderately hot	190/200	370/400	5/6
Hot	210/220	410/440	6/7
Very hot	230	450	8
Super hot	250/290	475/550	9/10

DRY MEASURES

Metric	Imperial
30 grams	1 ounce
45 grams	1 1/2 ounces
55 grams	2 ounces
70 grams	2 1/2 ounces
85 grams	3 ounces
100 grams	3 1/2 ounces
110 grams	4 ounces
125 grams	4 1/2 ounces
140 grams	5 ounces
280 grams	10 ounces
450 grams	16 ounces (1 pound)
500 grams	1 pound, 1 1/2 ounces
700 grams	1 1/2 pounds
800 grams	1 3/4 pounds
1 kilogram	2 pounds, 3 ounces
1.5 kilograms	3 pounds, 4 1/2 ounces
2 kilograms	4 pounds, 6 ounces

LENGTH

Metric	Imperial
0.5 cm	1/4 inch
1 cm	1/2 inch
1.5 cm	3/4 inch
2.5 cm	1 inch

ABBREVIATION

tsp	teaspoon
Tbsp	tablespoon
g	gram
kg	kilogram
ml	millilitre